WITHDRAWN

Silly Sketcher

Draw a Funny Alphabet!

written by Luke Colins

illustrated by Catherine Cates

**BLACK
RABBIT
BOOKS**

Hi Jinx is published by Black Rabbit Books
P.O. Box 3263, Mankato, Minnesota, 56002.
www.blackrabbitbooks.com
Copyright © 2020 Black Rabbit Books

Jennifer Besel, editor; Catherine Cates,
interior designer; Michael Sellner, cover designer;
Omay Ayres, photo researcher

Library of Congress Cataloging-in-Publication Data
Names: Colins, Luke, author.
Title: Draw a funny alphabet! / by Luke Colins.
Description: Mankato, Minnesota : Black Rabbit Books, [2020] |
Series: Hi jinx. Silly sketcher | Includes bibliographical references and
index. | Audience: Ages: 8-12. | Audience: Grades: 4 to 6
Identifiers: LCCN 2018039911 (print) | LCCN 2018061130 (ebook) |
ISBN 9781680729511 (ebook) | ISBN 9781680729450 (library binding) |
ISBN 9781644660706 (pbk.)
Subjects: LCSH: Alphabets—Juvenile literature. | Drawing—Technique—
Juvenile literature. | Alphabet—Juvenile literature.
Classification: LCC NK3630 (ebook) | LCC NK3630 .C65 2020 (print) |
DDC 745.6/1—dc23
LC record available at https://lccn.loc.gov/2018039911

Printed in China. 1/19

Image Credits

Alamy: Matthew Cole, 5; iStock: carbouval, 5; Shutterstock: anfisa focusova,
19; Designer things, 20; Mario Pantelic, Cover, Back Cover, 3, 5, 12, 15;
Memo Angeles, Cover, 4, 5, 6, 8–9, 11, 12–13, 15, 17, 19, 20, 23; Olga
Sabo, 2-3, 5; opicobello, 6, 15, 18; owatta, 5; ozzichka, 8–9; Pasko Maksim,
Back Cover, 9, 16, 23, 24; Pitju, 3, 9, 21; Ron Dale, 3, 4, 6, 7, 9, 11, 16,
18, 20; Tueris, 11 Every effort has been made to contact copyright holders
for material reproduced in this book. Any omissions will be rectified in
subsequent printings if notice is given to the publisher.

Contents

Chapter 1

Be a Silly Sketcher!

Words on a page can be really funny. But you can make those words even sillier. Adding eyes or squiggles can turn a word into art.

To be a silly sketcher, all you need is a pencil, some paper, and a funny bone. Draw a circle here. Add some swirls there. Just follow the steps. You'll have hilarious art in no time.

What You Need

pencils

pencil sharpener
(just in case)

lots of paper

eraser

colored pencils and markers

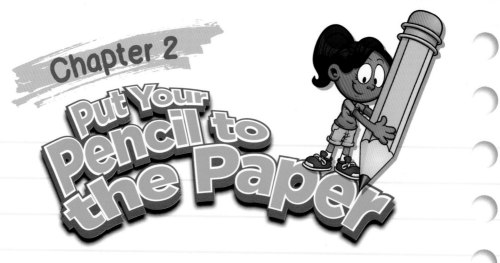

Chapter 2
Put Your Pencil to the Paper

Dots are a simple way to add something silly to your words. Give them a try!

Step 1

Write a phrase using blocky letters. Draw the letters lightly. You'll erase some of it later.

HAVE A GREAT DAY.

Step 2

Add small straight lines to
the ends of each letter.

HAVE A GREAT DAY.

Step 3

Put dots along the lines.
Do your best to space the
dots out evenly.

HAVE A GREAT DAY.

Step 4

Erase the lines between the dots.
Redraw any circles that might
have been erased.

HAVE A GREAT DAY.

Finish It Up!

Try shading the dots in
with colored pencils.

GREAT DAY

All Curled Up

Adding swirls can give your letters a special touch.

Step 1

Write the first letter of your word or phrase.

Step 2

Add swirls to the ends of the letter.

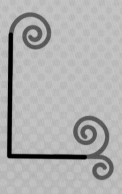

Step 3

Repeat steps 1 and 2 for the remaining letters in your word or phrase. For the letter O, put swirls in the middle. For other letters, draw swirls wherever they look best!

Flower Power

Let your words sprout with this fun alphabet.

Step 1
Draw the first letter in your word or phrase. Make it big, so there's room to add designs.

Step 2
Add swirled vines coming from the corners or straight lines.

Step 3
Add flower shapes **overlapping** the vines.

VALENTINE

Step 4

Draw teardrop shapes for leaves along the vines.

Step 5

Repeat steps 1 through 4 for the remaining letters in your word or phrase. Make straight lines into unopened **buds**. Use different flower shapes to make your letters stand out.

Finish It Up!

Glue dried flowers around the words for an added special touch.

Birthday Blowout

Bring some light into your birthday notes with these fun letters.

Step 1

Write the first letter of your word or phrase. Make it big, so there's room for decorations.

Step 2

Draw candles around any upright lines in the letter. Don't forget the flickering flames!

Step 3

Add **horizontal** swirls on top of lines that cross, such as on "H" or "t."

Step 4

Erase the lines you drew in step 1.

Step 5

Repeat steps 1 through 4 for the rest of the letters in your word or phrase.

Monster Mash

Bring your letters to life with this fun alphabet. You'll have everyone roaring with laughter.

Step 1

Write the first letter of your word or phrase. Make the letter rounded.

Step 2

Add an **outline** around the letter. Then add wiggling eyes. Finally, add hole details inside letters like "B" or "P."

Step 3

Erase the original letter.

Color a gooey looking shape around the word or phrase. Make it nice and drippy.

Step 4

Add details to the letter to make it look like a monster. Maybe make a line into a mouth with fangs. Add **pupils** and **motion** lines.

Step 5

Repeat steps 1 through 4 for the rest of the letters in your word or phrase. Be creative. Use **scalloped** lines to create fur. Use cones for horns. Do whatever looks funny!

Bubble Up

Big, fluffy bubble letters always make people smile. Try these silly letters next.

Step 1
Write the first letter of your word.

Step 2
Draw overlapping circles and ovals on top of the letter. The ovals and circles should follow the shape of the letter.

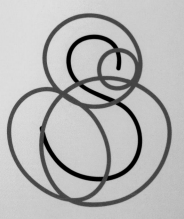

Finish It Up!

Try adding color **accents** inside the shapes. It will make them look like full balloons.

Step 3

Erase all the lines inside the overlapping shapes, including the letter you wrote in step 1.

Step 4

Repeat steps 1 though 3 for the remaining letters of your word. The circles and ovals should overlap other letters. When you erase the overlapping lines, it will look like some are behind others.

Cool Comin' At Ya

In real life, things close to your eye look larger. Things farther away look smaller. Trick the eye into thinking that's what you're doing with your words. Really make your letters pop off the page with this 3-D technique.

Step 1

Write a word using straight lines.

Step 2

Outline each letter. Add hole details inside letters like "O" or "P."

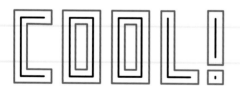

Tip

A ruler is a helpful tool for drawing straight lines.

Step 3

Erase the letters you drew in step 1. Add a dot centered above the word.

COOL!

Step 4

Draw straight lines from the dot to the outer corners of each letter. These lines will help you see where the next lines go.

Step 5

Use the straight lines to add accent lines to the letters. These are the lines that will make things really seem 3-D.

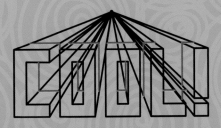

Step 6

Erase the lines that don't form parts of the 3-D letters.

Chapter 3

Get in on the Hi Jinx

Graphic artists use the same steps you just did! They start words with simple letters. Then they add details, such as 3-D lines and color. Their fun word art is all over the graphic novels we love to read. Maybe one day you'll draw a graphic novel!

Take It One Step More

1. Most of the drawings tell you to erase lines inside overlapping shapes. What happens if you skip that step?

2. Are your sketches more or less funny with color? Why?

3. Each project has you start by writing the letter first. Why is that a good place to start?

GLOSSARY

accent (AK-sent)—an emphasis put on part of a design

bud (BUHD)—a small growth on a plant that hasn't opened into a flower or leaf yet

horizontal (hor-uh-ZON-tuhl)—being parallel to the horizon

motion (MO-shun)—an act or process of moving

outline (AHWT-lyn)—to draw a line around the edges of something

overlap (oh-vur-LAP)—to extend over or past

pupil (PYU-pul)—the part of the eye that lets light in; in people, it's the round, black part of the eye.

scalloped (SKAH-lupd)—using a series of half circles

trace (TRAYS)—to copy something by following the lines or letters as seen through a transparent sheet on top

BOOKS

Huff, Abby. *Draw Your Own Lettering and Decorative Zendoodles.* Draw Your Own Zendoodles. North Mankato, MN: Capstone Press, 2017.

The Great Big Book of Amazing Creative Lettering. Heatherton Vic, Australia: Hinkler Books, 2017.

Warnaar, Dawn Nicole. *DIY Lettering.* Lake Forest, CA: Walter Foster Jr., 2016.

WEBSITES

Drawing for Kids
mocomi.com/fun/arts-crafts/drawing-for-kids/

How to Draw
www.hellokids.com/r_12/drawing-for-kids/

How to Draw Archive
www.artforkidshub.com/ how-to-draw/

Use markers to outline your drawings. Let the marker lines dry before coloring them in.

Colored pencils are a great tool for coloring in your letters. Layer a color over another for a cool blended effect.

Don't worry if your letters don't look exactly like the ones in this book! Art is all about creating your own thing. Just have fun!